Table of Content

Introduction

Chapter 1:

1: Understanding the mysterious mind:

2: Sowing seeds of opportunity:

Here are some ways to nurture this mindset:

1. Appreciate the preschool spirit:

2. Prune limiting beliefs:

3: Break through crystal walls:

2. Use conversion tools:

3. Build a Growth Mindset Oasis:

Seek inspiration from the sun:

1. Sharpen your pickaxe:

2. Decode the Treasure Map:

3. The thrill of digging:

Validate and refine your gem Test the water:

1: Discovering Earth's jewels:

2. Decoding the alchemist's code:

3. Delving into the treasure trove:

Competitive Landscapes :

Healthcare Paradise:

3. Solve the business puzzle:

Step one:

Step two:

Step Three:

Chapter 3:

1. Plan your route to El Dorado:

Your Goals Handbook:

Financial Forecasting:

2. The Alchemist's Mission:

3 Maize Labyrinth:

Chapter 4:

1. The Alchemist's Toolkit:

2 Build Your Digital Garden:

3. Stream Your Digital Network:

Chapter 5:

1. The Symphony of Victory:

2. The Interview Alchemist's Quest:

3. Cultivating the Innovation Oasis:

The Seed of Trust:

The Nurturing Sun:

The Fertile Soil:

Chapter 6:

1. Conquering money:

2. The Alchemist's Bazaar:

3. Building an Empire Brick by Brick:

Weaving Revenue Spells for Maximum Profit

Chapter 7:

1. Alchemist Network:

2. Navigator and lighthouse:

3. The Weaver's Web:

Chapter 8:

Phoenix Forge:

Warrior Mindset:

Build a support network:

1. The Entrepreneurial Adventure:

2. The Alchemist's Crucible:

3. The Navigator and the Storm:

Chapter 9:

1. Stagnation of stagnation:

2. Uncovering the market's gems:

Here are some unique tactics:

3. Giants of transformation:

Chapter 10:

1. From Consumer to Contributor:

Find a reason to give:

Beyond the obvious: Unique giving:

Symphony of Change:

2. Integrating Purpose with Profit:

3. Carve your mark on the time:

Conclusion:

Copyright © NAMPI JA 2024. All rights reserved.

Before this document is duplicated or reproduced in any manner, the publisher's consent must be gained. Therefore, the contents within can neither be stored electronically, transferred, nor kept in a database. Neither in Part nor full can the document be copied, scanned, faxed, or retained without approval from the publisher or creator.

Introduction

Mysterious Path to Prosperity **Revealed for entrepreneurs**

In a world where success seems shrouded in mystery and wealth can seem like an unattainable dream For many people, there are hidden paths waiting to be discovered. Welcome to the exciting journey to discover the secrets of wealth and success.

This book is an invitation to an extraordinary journey that combines ancient wisdom with modern strategies and ideas from the world's most successful people. It's a journey that challenges your perceptions, ignites your ambitions, and allows you to break free from limiting chains of thinking. Throughout the pages of the book, you will be immersed in the world of startups, where dreams come true. Learn the stories of some of the world's greatest visionaries and innovators and discover the basis of their success.

From humble beginnings to rapid advancement, their journey will inspire you to believe in endless possibilities. Get ready to explore an unexplored territory with lucrative business opportunities, where untapped potential lurks. We guide you through the industry maze and give you the tools to identify and pursue the most promising companies. With strategic thinking and steadfast determination, you can open the doors to wealth creation that was previously only accessible to a privileged few.

But this journey does not stop at accumulating wealth. It's about creating a legacy that goes beyond material wealth. We delve into the field of sales and marketing, where the art of persuasion and mastery of human psychology combine. Learn how to craft compelling stories, create authentic connections, and leave a lasting mark in the hearts and minds of your audience. On this winding road, we will encounter the foundation of success: a strong team and a thriving company culture.

Together, we will discover the secret to attracting the best talent, fostering collaboration and creating an environment conducive to growth and innovation. Your team will be your most valuable asset and will take you to unprecedented heights. However, the journey to wealth and success is not without challenges. We face inevitable obstacles and failures and turn them into stepping stones on the path to greatness. Failure is no longer a hindrance but a catalyst for growth, a beacon that leads you to resilience and unwavering determination.

Throughout this journey, we embrace the spirit of innovation and change, and innovative ideas have the power to transform industries and redefine standards. Learn to break conventions, ask questions and challenge the status quo. With this creative ingenuity, you can carve out a place for yourself in a world that craves innovation. But wealth and success are not the ultimate goal. These are just important milestones on a larger path. We explore the profound impact of giving, leaving a lasting legacy that goes beyond individual success.

Philanthropy and social responsibility will be the pillars on which you build your empire, ensuring that your wealth becomes a force for good in the world. So, my dear friends seeking prosperity, I invite you to join this extraordinary adventure. Discover the secrets that many have overlooked and unlock the untapped potential within you. Let's explore together the mysterious path to wealth and success, and create a rich, fulfilling, and truly extraordinary future.

Chapter 1:

The Magic of Entrepreneurship At the heart of every successful entrepreneur is a deep harmony, a subtle blend of thoughts, beliefs and perspectives that sets them apart from others. Ordinary businessmen. This chapter delves into the mysterious realm of entrepreneurship and reveals the secret to its extraordinary success. Prepare to embark on a transformational journey where the alchemy of the mind is the key to unlocking the immense potential within you.

We'll explore the complex workings of entrepreneurial psychology, peeling back the layers to uncover the fundamental elements that ignite the fire of prosperity. At the heart of this alchemy is an uncompromising belief in the infinite possibilities that exist in the world. We will challenge the limitations of limited thinking, allowing you to adopt a mindset of abundance and opportunity.

You will no longer be limited by chains of doubt and fear; Instead, you will move forward with unwavering confidence and a firm belief in your own abilities. But entrepreneurial thinking goes beyond mere belief: it's a never-ending quest to grow and learn.

We'll delve into the realm of continuous improvement, where every failure becomes a stepping stone to progress. With an insatiable thirst for knowledge and hunger for personal growth, you will cultivate a mindset that overcomes challenges, turning them into springboards to success.

However, the alchemy of the entrepreneurial mind is not just focused on personal gain; it stems from a deep sense of purpose and a desire to create meaningful impact. We will explore the power of passion and purpose, guiding you to discover your true calling and incorporate it into every aspect of your entrepreneurial journey. By aligning your actions with your core values, you will create a business that not only thrives, but also leaves a lasting legacy.

As we delve deeper into the mysteries of entrepreneurship, we will discover the art of resilience and adaptability. In the face of adversity and uncertainty, successful entrepreneurs demonstrate unwavering determination to persevere. We'll give you the tools you need to navigate the ever-changing business landscape, seeing challenges as opportunities to grow and innovate.

But perhaps the most profound aspect of entrepreneurship is the ability to envision a future that goes beyond the present. We will explore the power of imagination and visualisation, guiding you to create a clear, unambiguous vision of your desired outcome.

Through the alchemy of the mind, you will turn your dreams into reality and make them come true. So, dear readers, prepare to discover the secrets of entrepreneurship, a realm where faith inspires possibility, where growth flourishes amid challenges, and where purpose drives promote profound impact.

Embrace your inner chemistry and embark on a journey that will transform not just your business but your entire way of life. May your entrepreneurial spirit become the catalyst for your extraordinary success.

1: Understanding the mysterious mind:

The psychology of successful pioneers In the vast tapestry of human psychology, there exists a world for those who dare to dream, the those who defy convention and those who forge their own path. to prosperity.

This chapter is an invitation to delve into the entrepreneur's mind, unravelling the subtleties of its thoughts, feelings, and motivations. Prepare to embark on a journey of discovery that explores the inner workings of successful entrepreneurs. We will traverse lands of ambition, resilience and creativity, exploring the labyrinthine corridors of their minds.

At the heart of the entrepreneurial mentality is an unshakable belief in the power of possibility. We will venture into the realm of limitless thinking, where boundaries are broken and new frontiers are created. These visionaries possess an innate ability to see opportunities where others see obstacles, to imagine a future that transcends the present. Their minds are fertile ground for bold ideas and revolutionary innovations. But entrepreneurship is not without its challenges.

We will navigate the treacherous waters of fear, self-doubt, and uncertainty that often accompany the pursuit of success. These pioneers possess extraordinary resilience, a tenacity that fuels their determination to overcome failure and persevere in the face of adversity. Their spirit is bolstered by an unwavering belief in their own abilities and an unwavering commitment to their vision.

Creativity is also a characteristic of entrepreneurship. We will travel through the vast landscapes of the imagination, where innovative ideas form and flourish. These entrepreneurs possess a unique ability to push the boundaries of convention, challenge the status quo, and disrupt industries through their ingenuity. Their minds are fertile ground for bold experimentation and visionary thinking. However, the psychology of successful entrepreneurs goes beyond personal gain.

We will explore the profound impact of purpose and passion, delving deep into their hearts and minds. These pioneers were driven by a deep desire to make a meaningful difference in the world, leaving a lasting legacy that goes beyond material wealth.

Their spirit is driven by purpose and commitment to creating positive change. By exploring the mysterious psychology of successful entrepreneurs, we will uncover the complex dance between risk and reward.

These visionaries have a unique relationship with uncertainty, seeing it not as a threat but as an opportunity for growth and discovery. Their minds are endowed with calculated boldness, willing to take moderate risks in pursuit of their goals.

So, dear readers, prepare to immerse yourself in the captivating world of entrepreneurship, a world where boldness meets resilience, where creativity blends with purpose and where passion drives the quest for prosperity.

Grasp the nuances of their psychology and let their stories inspire and empower you on your own entrepreneurial journey. May their understanding of the mind become a catalyst to unlock the extraordinary potential within you.

2: Sowing seeds of opportunity:

Nurturing an entrepreneurial mindset. Think of wealth and opportunity not as fleeting butterflies to be pursued but as fertile seeds waiting to be nurtured nourishment. Cultivating an entrepreneurial mindset is not about capturing fleeting moments but about creating fertile ground where success can take root and flourish.

Here are some ways to nurture this mindset:

1. Appreciate the preschool spirit:

Curiosity is your water source: Like a seedling stretching toward the sunlight , cultivate endless curiosity. Ask questions, explore new ideas, and let your imagination run wild.

Knowledge is the food that nourishes your entrepreneurial spirit. Embrace the mess: Farming often involves digging and getting a little dirty. Don't be afraid to experiment, fail and learn from your mistakes. Every misstep is an opportunity to refine your approach and strengthen your roots.

2. Prune limiting beliefs:

Identify the weeds: Limiting beliefs, like stubborn weeds, can hold back your potential. Recognize your negative and limiting thoughts like "I'm not good enough" or "It's too risky. " Root out these weeds by replacing them with empowering affirmations. Look for the Sun: Surround yourself with positive influencers, mentors, and a community that supports your entrepreneurial journey. Their encouragement and sharing of experiences are like sunshine, promoting growth and confidence.

Nurture your ecosystem:
Collaboration is fertiliser: Teamwork turns dreams into reality. Build strong relationships with collaborators, partners and potential customers. By maintaining a supportive ecosystem, you create a network that helps your business thrive.

Return to the garden:
Remember that even the largest oak tree starts from a small seed. Share knowledge, mentor future entrepreneurs, and contribute to your community. By giving, you enrich the entire startup ecosystem, thereby accelerating the cycle of growth and prosperity. By adopting this "seeding mentality," you move from passively waiting for opportunities to actively creating fertile ground for them to grow.

Remember that wealth and success are not just destinations but journeys driven by a spirit of curiosity, perseverance and collaboration. So plant the seeds of your business vision, nurture them with the right mindset, and watch them grow into opportunities that will pay off for years to come.

3: Break through crystal walls:

Embrace growth and smash limiting beliefs Imagine your mind as a magnificent crystal palace. In its glittering rooms lie your dreams and aspirations, waiting to be unleashed. But alas, some rooms are surrounded by majestic crystal walls – these are your limiting beliefs. They whisper doubts, amplify fears, and hinder your potential. To reach your full potential, you must embark on a journey to break down these walls and embrace the limitless possibilities of a growth mindset.

1. **Unearth hidden walls:**

Silence echoing whispers: The first step is to become aware of these limiting beliefs. Pay attention to the negative self-talk that creeps into your mind. Do you tell yourself "I can't" or "I'm not good enough"? These are the whispers of crystal walls, seeking to envelop you. Question the foundation: Don't just accept these beliefs as truth. Challenge them! Are they based on truth or fear? Do they hold you back in the past? By questioning their authenticity, you begin to shake their foundation.

2. **Use conversion tools:**

The power of "re": Replace limiting statements with empowering statements. Instead of saying "I can't do that yet," say "I can't do that yet.
" This simple change acknowledges current limitations but opens the door to future possibilities through effort and learning.

The Reframing Hammer: Reframing challenges into opportunities for growth. See failures as stepping stones, not obstacles. By viewing difficulties as learning experiences, you pave the way for progress.

3. **Build a Growth Mindset Oasis:**

Seek inspiration from the sun: Surround yourself with positive influences and inspiring stories of individuals who have overcome their beliefs and similar limitations.

Their journey becomes a warm ray of sunshine that nourishes your growth mindset. Celebrate the smallest flowers: Acknowledge and celebrate each small victory and move forward. This reinforces the positive aspects of your growth journey and boosts your motivation to continue breaking through crystal walls. Remember that adopting a growth mindset is an ongoing journey, not a one-time event.

By continually challenging your limiting beliefs, using transformational tools, and surrounding yourself with positivity, you can escape the confines of your crystal palace and enter a world of infinite possibilities. The world is waiting for your unique shine, so go ahead, tear down those walls, and let your full potential come true!

Chapter 2:

Excavating Gemstones: Treasure Hunter's Guide to Lucrative Business Opportunities
Welcome, Intrepid Explorer! Buckle up and embark on an exciting expedition to discover the hidden gems of the business world - lucrative opportunities waiting to be discovered. In this chapter, we will equip you with the tools and mindset of a treasure hunter, transforming you from a passive observer to an active seeker of business wealth.

1. Sharpen your pickaxe:

Cultivate a keen eye for opportunities Inspire the spirit of discovery: Curiosity is your compass. Explore diverse industries, listen to customer pain points, and identify unmet needs. Be a relentless questioner, always looking for gaps and inefficiencies that can be filled with creative solutions. Make friends with the locals: Immerse yourself in your target market. Understand their needs, wants, and pain points. Talk to potential customers, observe their behaviour and analyse existing trends. This local knowledge becomes your treasure map, guiding you to hidden opportunities.

2. Decode the Treasure Map:

Analyse trends and identify gaps Monitor the whispers of change: Stay on top of emerging trends in technology, demographics and social consciousness. These trends act like whispers, hinting at changes in consumer preferences and potential disruptions to established markets.

Unearth hidden gaps: Look beyond the surface and identify unmet needs or inefficiencies in existing industries. Can you come up with a more sustainable, more practical or more personalised solution? By identifying these gaps, you will uncover hidden opportunities waiting to be exploited.

3. The thrill of digging:

Validate and refine your gem Test the water: Don't just dream; experience! Develop a minimum viable product (MVP) and test it with a small group of potential customers. Collect feedback, iterate based on their needs, and refine your product until it really shines. Assess market potential: Research the size and growth potential of your target market. Is there enough demand to support your business?

Understanding market dynamics helps assess the potential value of your discovered gem. Remember that the journey to discovering profitable business opportunities is an adventure, not a destination. Enjoy the thrill of discovery, continuously hone your skills and never stop searching.

With the right tools, mindset, and a little spirit of discovery, you'll be on your way to unearthing hidden gems waiting to be turned into thriving businesses.

1: Discovering Earth's jewels:

The quest for greatness Our planet, a living tapestry woven of diverse landscapes and cultures, filled with hidden treasures.

To embark on a journey in search of the world's greatest is to step through a portal, leave the mundane behind and enter a realm of awe-inspiring wonder. Imagine crossing the sunlit plains of Africa, where vast herds thunder across the savannah, their primordial energy echoing through the ages.

Witness the heavenly ballet of the Northern Lights, their emerald and purple hues painting the night sky with incredible brilliance. Immerse yourself in the emerald heart of the Amazon rainforest, where ancient giants pierce the sky and the symphony of life hums in every rustle of leaves. The greatest things in the world are not limited to the natural realm.

Explore the labyrinthine streets of ancient cities, where whispers of history linger in every crumbling arch and weathered rock. Climb to the top of a towering man-made wonder, whose intricate details are a testament to human ingenuity and perseverance.

Stand humbly before the quiet canvas of a masterpiece, its strokes capturing the essence of an era, a culture, a soul. This mission is about more than just collecting unique souvenirs. It's about pushing the boundaries of your perception, breaking stereotypes and embracing the kaleidoscopic experiences our world has to offer. It's about creating connection – with breathtaking landscapes, vibrant cultures and the indomitable spirit that resides in us all.

2. Decoding the alchemist's code:

Revealing the magic of business The world of entrepreneurs is a captivating landscape where dreams soar and turn into empires. These individuals, modern-day alchemists, possess a unique blend of vision, courage, and a touch of daring. Their story is not simply a chronicle of success; they are complex woven with innovation, resilience, and occasional mistakes, becoming springboards to greatness.

Imagine venturing into the bustling marketplace of ideas where these alchemists, eyes sparkling with possibility, weave their magic. Witness, in the quiet hum of a garage, the birth of a technological wonder that will reshape our world.

Witness, amidst the chaos of a rapidly growing startup, the relentless determination of a team pursuing a seemingly impossible dream. Their story is not a fairy tale with a guaranteed happy ending. They are full of pitfalls, moments of doubt, and the ever-present risk of failure.

But it is in these struggles that their great nature lies. They are phoenixes, rising from the ashes of their failures, their wings carrying wisdom gleaned from experience. Exploring the world of these entrepreneurs isn't just about marvelling at their success.

It's about deciphering the alchemist's code, the fundamentals that drove their journey. It's about learning from their failures, understanding that the path to greatness is rarely a straight line.

So, embark on this intellectual adventure, dear researcher. Dive into the annals of these visionaries, not only to inspire you but also to equip yourself. Because in their stories lie the secrets that will allow you to unleash your own entrepreneurial spirit, the ability to make your dreams come true and leave your own indelible mark on the global landscape. Demand is always changing.

3. Delving into the treasure trove:

Unearthing industries poised to thrive Imagine yourself as an intrepid explorer, navigating a vast landscape of industries, each one a hidden valley filled with riches.

Your trusted tag: , an analytical framework for identifying the sectors most likely to create wealth. To embark on this exciting mission, buckle up and equip yourself with these important tools: Cartographer's compass: Identify growth drivers: Find that The industry is driven by strong tailwinds, such as technological advances driving artificial intelligence or demographic shifts driving growth. Demand for elderly care solutions.

Competitive Landscapes :

Terrain exploration. Are there dominant players or is it a fragmented market ripe for disruption? Barriers to entry: Is the treasure protected by high upfront costs, complex regulations or specialised knowledge? Lower barriers mean easier access to potential benefits. Unearthing gems:

Now let's look at specific industries that could hold the key to prosperity: Sustainability oases: The clean energy sector is booming, due to the global need to combat climate change. Renewable energy sources such as solar and wind are poised for significant growth. Digital Frontier: The technology landscape continues to evolve at a breakneck pace. Artificial intelligence, cybersecurity and metadata are just some of the areas with huge potential for innovation and wealth creation.

Healthcare Paradise:

The healthcare industry is constantly adapting to meet the ageing population and growing healthcare needs. Fields such as personalised medicine, biotechnology and telemedicine promise future growth.

Dear adventurer, remember that wealth creation is not without risk. Do your research thoroughly, diversify your investments and seek professional advice before venturing into new territory.

Beyond the Map: This is just the starting point. The real treasure lies in continually honing your analytical skills, staying informed about emerging trends, and adapting your strategy to the ever-changing economic landscape. With a little curiosity, a little caution, and a little calculated risk, you can embark on an exciting journey to wealth creation, one insightful analysis at a time.

3. Solve the business puzzle:

Exploit profitable opportunities The world of business is a vast puzzle, full of hidden pieces that when put together correctly reveal a picture of enormous success. You, an intrepid entrepreneur, are searching for the elusive pieces of the puzzle – the lucrative opportunities that are lying dormant, waiting to be unearthed. Here's your decoding round to solve the business puzzle:

Step one:

Become a master detective: Hone your observation skills: The world is a treasure trove of clues. Listen to customer frustrations, observe inefficiencies in existing systems, and identify unmet needs. Leaky faucets aren't just a plumbing problem; This could signal a new water-saving innovation. Embrace the Art of Curiosity: Challenge the Status Quo. Why do we do things this way? Is there a better, faster or more cost-effective solution? Curiosity is the spark that sparks creative ideas.

Step two:

Decoding the market landscape: Befriending the data dragon: Market research is your loyal companion. Collect data on target demographics, competitor analysis, and industry trends. This information will light the way for a viable business idea.

Conduct a conversation with a customer: Don't make assumptions. Talk to your potential customers! Understand their problems, desires and buying habits. These conversations will shape your product or service to perfectly meet market needs.

Step Three:

Put together the profitability puzzle: Financial forecast: Every good detective needs a plan. Develop a financial forecast that estimates your initial costs, expected revenue, and potential profits. This ensures that your great idea is also financially viable. SWOT Spotlight: Highlight your strengths, weaknesses, opportunities and threats (SWOT analysis).

Understanding your competitive advantages and potential obstacles will help you navigate your strategy within the business landscape. Remember that an entrepreneur's journey is rarely linear. Be prepared to adjust your approach as you gather new information. With a keen eye for opportunity, a thirst for knowledge and a calculated dose of risk, you'll be well placed to tackle tough business questions and discover the lucrative opportunities that await. Friend!

Chapter 3:

Forging the unbreakable pillars of success Imagine you are embarking on a grand architectural project, not with bricks and mortar but self-development. This chapter serves as your blueprint, guiding you to build a solid foundation for personal and professional achievements.

The foundation of clarity: The first pillar of your success is clarity. Just like an architect meticulously draws up a building design, you need to clearly define your goals and aspirations. What do you aspire to achieve? What legacy do you want to leave behind? Excavating the

Foundations of Self-Awareness: Next, let's delve into the fertile ground of self-awareness. Understand your strengths and weaknesses, values and motivations. This introspection allows you to identify areas of growth and take advantage of your natural talents.

Knowledge and Skills Pillar: Now the construction begins. Gain the necessary knowledge and skills to make your dreams come true. Find a mentor, research educational resources, and practice tirelessly. Remember, knowledge is the mortar that holds your foundations together and skills are the steel that strengthens them.

Resilient Building: The road to success is rarely paved with smooth stones. Expect challenges and failures. However, cultivate resilience. Learn from your mistakes, bounce back from each stumble, and never let adversity stop you from your mission. The eternal boat of continuous learning:

Finally, remember that building your success is not a one-time project. Accept continuous learning. Stay informed about advances in your field, explore new ideas, and adjust your approach as needed. This lifelong learning journey ensures your foundation remains strong and adaptable in the ever-changing landscape of life. With these pillars firmly placed, you have built a foundation stronger than any fortress.

This will help you weather any storm And motivate you to achieve your greatest ambitions. So, embark on this journey of self-discovery and self-building, and watch your potential transform into a remarkable achievement.

1. **Plan your route to El Dorado**:

The Navigator's Guide to Effective Business Planning and Strategy Imagine that you are an intrepid explorer, setting out on a journey to the legendary town of El Dorado, a land of opportunity. and success. Your trusted ship? A carefully crafted business plan and strategy, a map and compass to guide you through uncharted territories.

Your Goals Handbook:

A solid business plan serves as a constitution, outlining your business goals, much like chartering a ship sets the course and purpose for your business. It. It clearly articulates your mission statement, a statement of your company's core values and aspirations. This guiding principle ensures that your team, both employees and stakeholders, remains engaged and motivated.

Mapping the market landscape: Next, unfold the complex market analysis – a detailed map of your business terrain. It reveals your industry terrain, identifying your target audience, potential competitors, and dominant market trends. Understanding these forces allows you to direct currents and avoid dangerous shoals.

Financial Forecasting:

Charting the Path to Prosperity: No journey is complete without reliable financial forecasts. This important document serves as your compass, charting the path to financial stability. He meticulously estimates initial costs, expected revenue streams, and potential profits. With this financial roadmap, you can make informed decisions about your resource allocation and investment strategy.

Follow the changing winds: Remember that the sea is rarely calm. Your strategic plan is the sail that keeps you moving forward, even when unforeseen storms arise. It describes your marketing strategies to reach your target audience, your operational plans to ensure efficient production and distribution, and contingency plans to adapt to market conditions. school.

The School is changing. This adaptability allows you to adjust your sails and meet unforeseen challenges. The endless refinement journey: Think of your business plan and strategy as a living document, not a static one. As you gather market data and encounter new opportunities, be prepared to refine and update your plan regularly.

This continuous improvement ensures your journey stays on track and adapts to the ever-changing business landscape. With a solid business plan and a strategic compass in hand, you are well equipped to navigate the uncharted waters of the business world. So get on board, brave entrepreneurs, and chart your course towards the El Dorado of success!

2. The Alchemist's Mission:

Turn dreams into funded projects Imagine that you are an alchemist, working not with cup and fire but with ideas and ambitions. Your goal? To transform your business vision from a simple base metal with potential into the shining gold of a funded business. This unique journey requires you to master the art of attracting investment and here is your guide to becoming a master alchemist:

Know yourself and your business: Before you embark On your research journey, learn more about yourself. Understand the nature of your business: unique value proposition, market potential and competitive landscape. This self-awareness is the foundation on which you build your compelling story.

Craft the Philosopher's Stone: Playground: Your playground is the Philosopher's Stone, the key ingredient that unlocks investment potential. It should be a compelling story that highlights your company's potential to generate significant profits.

Create a story that sparks investors' imaginations, highlights the problem your company solves, the market opportunity it addresses, and the experienced team behind it. Finding the right investor: Not all investors are the same. Research and identify investors suitable for your industry and stage of development.

Venture capitalists may be attracted to high-growth startups, while angel investors may back companies with social impact. Finding a compatible partner will increase your chances of success.

Alchemist's tools: Financial forecasting and due diligence: Investors themselves are not alchemists; they are based on cold, concrete facts. Prepare solid financial projections to demonstrate your business's profitability potential. Be prepared to go through due diligence, a process in which investors thoroughly examine your finances, team, and market strategy.

Transparency and careful preparation are essential. Conversion: Negotiate and close the deal: Negotiating investment terms is the final step in your alchemical journey.

Approach it clearly and professionally, ensuring the deal benefits you and the investor. Remember that successful negotiation is not a zero-sum game; it's about building mutually beneficial partnerships.

Remember that an alchemist's quest is not always linear. Prepare for failures and adjust your approach if necessary. With a compelling vision, good presentation, and unwavering dedication, you can turn your business dreams into reality, one funded business at a time..

3 **Maize Labyrinth**:

Navigating the legal and regulatory landscape of business Imagine you are a daring explorer venturing into a labyrinth maze, not by stone and brick, but legal and regulatory complexity.

This complex web, so vital to any entrepreneur, holds both treasures and pitfalls. Here's a compass and guide to help you navigate this difficult terrain: Draw a route: Understand the legal landscape:

The first step is to map the landscape. Become familiar with the legal structures available for your business, such as a sole proprietorship or corporation. Each structure has its own tax implications and liability protections.

Consulting with a legal professional can help you choose the most suitable path for your business. Beware the Minotaur: Intellectual Property: The treasure in the maze lies in the form of intellectual property (IP), such as trademarks, patents, and copyrights. These rights protect your unique creations, like your brand name or product design.

Understanding intellectual property laws and obtaining proper registration will protect your assets from infringement. Navigating Dangerous Waters: Licences and Permits: Some industries require specific licences and permits to operate.

These regulations, while they may seem intimidating, often ensure consumer safety and fair competition. Seeking and obtaining the necessary licences demonstrates your commitment to compliance and responsible business practices..

The ever-changing sand: Staying compliant with regulations: The legal and regulatory landscape is not static. New rules and changes are constantly appearing. Staying informed through industry publications, regulatory advisors or government websites is essential to avoid errors and ensure your business remains compliant.

Build collaborative bridges: Seek professional advice: Don't try to get through this maze alone. Consulting with an experienced legal professional is invaluable. They can guide you through complex legal procedures, draft contracts and represent you in the event of a dispute.

This partnership bridges the gap between your business vision and the complexity of the legal world. Remember that the journey through the legal and regulatory maze is not a sprint but a marathon. With the right preparation, knowledge and guidance, you can solve complex problems and win, ready to build your business dreams on a solid legal and regulatory foundation

Chapter 4:

The Symphony of Persuasion: Mastering the Art of Sales and Marketing Imagine yourself as a master, using not a stick but sales tools merchandise and marketing. Your orchestra?.

A symphony of strategies designed to engage your audience and lead them on a conversion journey. This chapter serves as a soundtrack, guiding you in composing a harmonious blend of sales and marketing techniques.

The Overture: Understanding Your Audience:

Before the first note is played, a successful maestro must know their audience. In the world of sales and marketing, this translates to deep customer understanding. Who are you trying to reach? What are their needs, desires, and pain points? By conducting thorough market research and leveraging customer data, you can tailor your message to resonate with their specific interests.

The Melody of Storytelling:

People connect with stories. Craft a compelling narrative that showcases your product or service as the hero, solving the customer's challenges and leading them to a happy ending. Use emotional language, vivid imagery, and powerful testimonials to weave a captivating tale that resonates on a deeper level.

The Harmony of Integrated Strategies:
Your sales and marketing efforts shouldn't exist in separate silos. They should complement and amplify each other, creating a harmonious whole. Leverage social media marketing to generate brand awareness and drive traffic to your website, where compelling sales copy and targeted calls to action convert visitors into customers.

The Rhythm of Content Marketing:
In today's digital age, content is king. Create valuable and informative content, such as blog posts, webinars, or infographics, that educates your audience and establishes you as a thought leader in your industry. This content not only attracts potential customers but also nurtures existing relationships, fostering brand loyalty.

The Virtuosity of Building Relationships:
At the heart of successful sales and marketing lies the art of building relationships. Develop genuine connections with your customers, not just transactions. Listen to their concerns, address their questions, and personalise your interactions. This fosters trust and loyalty, turning customers into brand advocates.

The Encore: Continuous Improvement:
Remember, the music of sales and marketing never truly ends. Analyse your results regularly, track key metrics, and adapt your strategies based on data insights. Be willing to experiment with new tactics and embrace continuous improvement to ensure your symphony of persuasion remains captivating and effective.

By following this musical score, you can master the art of sales and marketing, transforming your audience from passive listeners into active participants in your brand's success story. So, step onto the stage, raise your metaphorical baton, and conduct your symphony of persuasion to a chorus of resounding conversions.

1. The Alchemist's Toolkit:

Effective Sales and Marketing Techniques for Entrepreneurial Glory
Imagine yourself as a cunning alchemist, not brewing potions, but concocting potent elixirs of sales and marketing magic. These elixirs, wielded by successful entrepreneurs, transform a simple idea into a customer-enchanting product and a fledgling business into a thriving enterprise.

Here's a peek into the alchemist's toolkit:
The Philosopher's Stone: The Power of Storytelling
People don't buy products; they buy stories. Successful entrepreneurs are master storytellers. They weave compelling narratives that position their product as the hero, vanquishing the customer's villainous problems and ushering in a happy ending of convenience, happiness, or success.

This emotional connection resonates far deeper than dry product specifications.
The Universal Solvent: Understanding Your Audience
Before brewing any elixir, a skilled alchemist must understand the elements. Similarly, effective sales and marketing require a deep understanding of your target audience. Who are you trying to reach? What are their deepest desires and most pressing challenges? By wielding the power of market research and customer data, you can tailor your message to resonate with their specific needs.

The Amplification Charm: The Magic of Integrated Strategies

Sales and marketing shouldn't exist in separate cauldrons. They should be combined in a synergistic potion for maximum effect. Imagine leveraging social media to cast a spell of brand awareness, drawing potential customers towards your website.

There, compelling sales copy and irresistible calls to action act as a persuasive lure, turning visitors into loyal customers. The Cloak of Invisibility: The Appeal of Content Marketing In today's digital age, valuable content is the ultimate invisibility cloak, helping you become a trusted advisor in Your business. your field.

By creating informative content – blog posts like how to make bubbly or webinars as engaging as tornadoes – you educate your audience and position yourself as a leader about ideology. This helps you become a trusted expert, not just a salesman.

Empathy Amplifier: The Art of Building Relationships The heart of alchemy lies not only in potions but also in the subtle art of understanding the natural world. Likewise, successful entrepreneurs understand the importance of building genuine relationships with their customers. They don't just make transactions; they foster trust and loyalty by truly listening to concerns, answering questions carefully, and personalising every interaction.

This emotional chemistry turns customers into brand advocates, your most powerful marketing potion. The Philosopher's Mercury: The Power of Continuous Improvement The alchemist never stopped refining his formulas. Likewise, successful entrepreneurs adopt a growth mindset.

They continuously analyse results, track key metrics like a prudent poison master, and adjust their strategies based on data. This willingness to experiment and innovate ensures that their marketing and sales magic stays strong, attracting new customers and keeping them captivated.

By using these alchemy tools, you too can develop a successful sales and marketing strategy, turning your business from a simple idea into a customer-happy success story . So, light your business fire, gather the ingredients and start your journey to brew the most powerful elixirs for sales and marketing magic!

2 Build Your Digital Garden:

Build a thriving online presence and personal brand Imagine you're not a bricks and mortar builder but a grower Cultivate a vibrant digital garden.

In this fertile landscape, you'll seed your unique talents, nurture them with engaging content, and watch your personal brand grow into a thriving online presence. Understanding Soil: Self-awareness is key Before planting anything, a trained gardener will evaluate the soil. Likewise, building a strong online presence starts with self-awareness.

What are your strengths and passions? What value can you bring to the virtual world? By understanding your unique qualities, you can choose the right seed – the content that most authentically resonates with you and your audience. Planting the Seed: Content is King Your content works like the seeds you plant in your digital garden.

It can be as diverse as colourful flowers: informative blog posts, engaging videos, insightful social media commentary, or even engaging podcasts. Remember, consistency is key. Regularly infuse your content with new ideas and compelling storytelling to ensure success.

Maintaining Flowers: Building Relationships Just as a gardener tends the land, nurturing connections is vital to your online presence. Interact with your audience, respond to comments, participate in relevant online discussions, and collaborate with others in your field. These interactions are like sunshine, nurturing your online garden and cultivating a sense of community around your brand.

Prune carefully: Maintain a positive image Just as a gardener carefully removes weeds, keep an eye on quality in organising your online presence. Pay attention to the content you share and the platforms you join. Remember that your online presence reflects your personal brand, so cultivate a positive and professional image.

Embrace the Seasons: Adapt and Evolve The online landscape is constantly evolving, just as the seasons change. Be willing to adapt and grow with them. Stay informed about emerging trends, explore new platforms, and refine your approach based on what resonates with your audience.

Remember, the most successful digital gardens are those that continually bloom.

tending Your digital garden with these essential elements, you can create a strong personal brand and online presence that stands out in a cluttered virtual world. So grab your virtual gardening tools, plant the seeds of your unique talent, and watch your personal brand bloom!

3. Stream Your Digital Network:

Reach a Wider Audience Through Social Media and the Magic of Marketing Imagine you're an experienced fisherman, broadcasting your Fishing Line located not in the physical ocean but in the vast digital sea of social media and online platforms. . Your bait?

Compelling content and strategic marketing techniques. Your goal? Attract a growing and engaged audience. Here's a fisherman's guide to conquering the digital waters: Know your catch: Know your prey Before casting a net, an experienced fisherman will do a meticulous study of the sea . Likewise, in the digital realm, success starts with understanding your audience.

Who are you trying to reach? What are their interests, online habits and preferred platforms? By conducting in-depth market research and leveraging audience insights, you can tailor your content and strategy to meet their specific needs. The Lure: Create Compelling Content Your content is the bait, the irresistible lure to attract your audience.

In the digital ocean, this attraction can take many forms: informative blog posts like writhing worms, captivating videos like schools of sparkling fish, or engaging posts on Social networks are like sparkling prey. Remember that quality and consistency are key.

Regularly create new and engaging content to keep your audience engaged and coming back for more. Casting the right net: Choosing the perfect platform Not all fishing nets are equal and neither are social media platforms. Explore the digital landscape and identify the platforms your target audience spends time on.

Are they lurking on the professional shores of LinkedIn or are they more likely to be found in the dazzling reefs of Instagram? Choose the platform that offers the best opportunity to connect with your audience. The Art of Story: Engage and Engage Once you've introduced your product line and gained attention, it's time to engage your audience.

Engage with them in a meaningful way. Respond to comments, join the conversation, and host live sessions or Q&A topics. This interaction fosters a sense of community and keeps your audience engaged, ensuring they don't float away like a slippery fish. Beyond Fishing: Use Paid Ads Sometimes, even the most experienced anglers need a little extra help.

Paid advertising options on social media platforms and search engines can serve as powerful accelerators, pushing your content further and reaching a wider audience. However, remember that targeted advertising is essential.

Use data and analytics to make sure your ads reach the right people at the right time. By using these digital fishing tools and strategies, you can cast your net effectively, attract a larger audience, and cultivate a community of followers who are engaged with your brand or brand. your brand. Your goals. So, venture into the digital sea, equip yourself with the right bait and prepare to witness the magic of social media and marketing!

Chapter 5:

Forging the Unbreakable: Creating a Winning Team and Company Culture Imagine that you are not a stone carver but a skilled blacksmith, forging The essential elements of a winning team and business culture. Your tools are not hammer and scissors but communication, collaboration and a shared vision.

Remember showstopper? A company where people flourish, and cooperation moves collective victory.

The Cauldron of Clarity:

Characterising Your Mission and Values

The primary step is to light the heater with a clear mission and set of values.

What is your company's reason? What centre standards direct your decision-making? When everybody gets the "why" behind the work, it cultivates a sense of solidarity and reason, the establishment upon which a solid group culture is built.

Gathering the Combination:

Building a Different and Gifted Group

Fair as a solid combination requires a mix of diverse metals, your group thrives with differing qualities. Look for people with changed foundations, encounters, and viewpoints. This cooperative energy of minds sparkles advancement, cultivates inventiveness, and leads to well-rounded arrangements.

The Craftsmanship of Communication:
Cultivating Open Exchange
Viable communication is the flux that ties your group together. Energize open and fair exchange, where everybody feels listened and esteemed. Make secure spaces for criticism, both positive and helpful. This straightforwardness cultivates believe, collaboration, and a sense of mental security, permitting your group to reach their full potential.

Engaging the Person:
Recognizing and Fulfilling Commitments
Fair as a metalworker recognizes the expertise of each pound blow, recognize and remunerate person commitments. Celebrate points of reference, both huge and little.

Give openings for professional development and development. This acknowledgment powers inspiration, cultivates a sense of achievement, and reinforces the individual's commitment to the team's victory.

The Unbreakable Soul:
Building Strength and Overcoming Challenges
No travel is without its cinders and sparkles. As a group, you'll unavoidably confront challenges. Be that as it may, by cultivating a culture of flexibility, you'll overcome impediments together. Empower shared back, celebrate "learning minutes" from misfortunes, and adjust your approach as required. This shared soul of tirelessness fortifies the team's bond and clears the way for long-term victory.

Keep in mind, building a winning group and company culture is a continuous prepare, not a one-time occasion. Persistently refine your approach, grasp criticism, and celebrate your collective achievements. With devotion and these essential components in hand, you'll produce a group that's not fair solid, but unbreakable. As your company advances, your group culture will serve as the strong establishment upon which you proceed to construct and accomplish enduring victory.

1. The Symphony of Victory:

The Concordant Part of a Solid Group in Entrepreneurial Triumph
Envision yourself not as a single conductor, but as the maestro of a grand orchestra – your entrepreneurial wander. Whereas you set the course and vision, the genuine enchantment lies within the agreeable collaboration of your group individuals, each a virtuoso in their claim right. Their combined talents, much just like the disobedient in a ensemble, weave a ensemble of success.

The Symphony of Qualities:

A solid group isn't almost about person brilliance; it's around complementing skillsets. Fair as violins and cellos mix to form a wealthy soundscape, your group ought to have a differences of qualities.

Look for people who exceed expectations in numerous zones, from promoting protesters to expository wizards and tech-savvy engineers. This cooperative energy of abilities ensures a well-rounded approach to exploring the complexities of your wander.

The Beat of Communication:
Open and compelling communication is the backbone of your group orchestra. Energize genuine discourse, where thoughts can be openly traded, concerns tended to, and input promptly given. This straightforward communication cultivates believe, decreases mistaken assumptions, and permits the group to work towards common objectives in idealize agreement.

The Tune of Inspiration:

A spurred group could be a effective constrain, moving your wonder forward. Cultivate a culture that recognizes and rewards person commitments, both enormous and little. Celebrate breakthroughs, offer openings for proficient advancement, and create a sense of reason by adjusting person objectives with the company's vision.

This acknowledgment fills energy, empowers possession, and keeps the group playing in idealize tune.

The Agreement of Versatility:

The entrepreneurial travel is seldom a smooth concerto. There will be disharmony and strife in the shape of challenges and difficulties. Be that as it may, a strong group, much like an ensemble usual to startling beat changes, has the versatility to overcome adversity. Encourage shared bolster, learn from botches, and adjust your approach as required.

This collective soul guarantees the music proceeds, indeed in the midst of unexpected disturbances.

The Fantastic Finale:

A Shared Triumph

Remember, building a solid team may be a ceaseless handle, associated with idealising the perplexing harmonies of a symphony. It requires devotion, steady hone, and a readiness to adjust.

By cultivating a culture of collaboration, communication, inspiration, and versatility, you enable your group individuals to end up genuine virtuosos, and together, make an ensemble of victory that reverberates with resonating commendation. As your wander takes centre stage, keep in mind, it's the concordant execution of your group that brings the shade down on a triumphant execution.

2. The Interview Alchemist's Quest:

Attracting, Hiring, and Retaining the Entrepreneurial El Dorado

Imagine yourself not as a recruiter, but as an alchemist, on a quest to transmute ordinary individuals into the shining gold of top talent.

Your laboratory is the recruitment process, and your tools are a blend of captivating strategies designed to attract, hire, and retain the most exceptional individuals for your entrepreneurial venture.

The Philosopher's Stone: Crafting a Compelling Employer Brand

Before embarking on your quest, you must craft your philosopher's stone: a compelling employer brand.

This brand isn't just about flashy logos or catchy slogans; it's about your company's core values, unique culture, and the impact you create. Showcase your mission, highlight your commitment to employee well-being and growth, and let your passion for your venture shine through. This authenticity resonates with and attracts individuals who share your vision and values.

The Universal Solvent: Understanding Your Talent Needs

Just as an alchemist wouldn't blindly search for any element, you need to understand your specific talent needs. Identify the skills, experience, and cultural fit crucial for each role within your venture. This clarity ensures you attract individuals who possess the right ingredients to contribute meaningfully and excel in their positions.

The Transmutation Chamber: The Art of the Interview

The interview transforms hopeful candidates into potential alchemists. Craft captivating interview experiences that go beyond rote questions and resumes.

Use scenario-based assessments, problem-solving exercises, and open-ended discussions to unveil not just technical skills, but also an individual's creativity, problem-solving abilities, and cultural fit.

The Elixir of Retention: Fostering Growth and Development

Retaining top talent is like perfecting the philosopher's stone – an ongoing process. Offer opportunities for continuous learning and professional development.

Provide mentorship programs, encourage participation in conferences and workshops, and invest in your employees' growth. This demonstrates your commitment to their long-term success and fosters a sense of loyalty and belonging.

The Philosopher's Mercury: Adapting and Refining

The landscape of talent is ever-evolving. Be prepared to adapt and refine your strategies. Utilise data and feedback from your recruitment process to identify areas for improvement. Stay updated on industry trends in talent acquisition and compensation packages.

This adaptability ensures you remain an attractive option for the top talent seeking to contribute to a thriving and evolving venture.

Remember, the alchemist's quest is not a solitary endeavour. Collaborate with other leaders within your organisation to create a unified and engaging recruitment experience.

By applying these alchemical strategies, you can attract, hire, and retain the exceptional individuals who will turn your entrepreneurial vision into a shining reality. So, embark on your quest, master the art of talent acquisition, and witness the alchemy that transforms individuals into the cornerstones of your entrepreneurial success.

3. **Cultivating the Innovation Oasis:**

Fostering Growth and Creativity in Your Company Culture

Imagine your company culture not as a rigid office environment, but as a vibrant oasis, where creativity blossoms, ideas flourish, and innovation thrives. This oasis is not built with brick and mortar, but with the following elements:

The Seed of Trust:

Building Open Communication

The first seed you sow is trust. Foster open communication where employees feel comfortable sharing ideas, voicing concerns, and offering constructive criticism.

Encourage transparent leadership, keeping employees informed and involved in decision-making processes. This open dialogue fosters a sense of psychological safety, allowing individuals to take calculated risks and experiment without fear of judgement.

The Nurturing Sun:

Celebrating and Rewarding Innovation doesn't thrive in the shade. Shine a light on creativity and initiative. Recognize and reward individuals and teams who go beyond the expected, who experiment with new approaches, and who challenge the status quo.

This recognition fuels motivation and sends a powerful message: "Innovation is valued here."

The Fertile Soil:

Embracing Diversity and Inclusion
A monoculture garden yields limited results. In your oasis, embrace diversity and inclusion. Cultivate a workforce with varied backgrounds, experiences, and perspectives. This synergy of minds sparks new ideas, fosters creative problem-solving, and leads to well-rounded solutions.

By valuing diverse voices and experiences, you tap into a wider wellspring of innovation.
The Watering Can of Collaboration:
Just as a lone plant struggles, innovation thrives through collaboration. Encourage cross-functional teams, where individuals from different departments come together to tackle challenges and exchange ideas.

Utilise collaborative tools, brainstorming sessions, and open project spaces to foster teamwork and break down silos. This cross-pollination of ideas leads to unexpected breakthroughs and innovative solutions.

The Weeding Tool of Constructive Feedback:
No oasis is perfect. Just as a gardener removes weeds, embrace constructive feedback. Encourage open and honest communication, where feedback is given and received respectfully and with the intent to improve.

This feedback loop allows individuals and teams to learn from mistakes, refine ideas, and continuously iterate towards innovative solutions.

Remember, cultivating an innovation oasis is an ongoing process, not a one-time event. Stay committed to fostering trust, celebrating innovation, embracing diversity, encouraging collaboration, and providing constructive feedback.

With these elements in place, your company culture will become a fertile ground for creativity, where growth and innovation blossom, propelling your business towards continued success. So, be the gardener of your company culture, and watch your oasis of innovation flourish!

Chapter 6:

The Alchemist's Forge - Turning Time into Gold Forget the Philosopher's Stone, the real magic lies in mastering the art of financial alchemy. In this chapter, we embark on the quest to transform the metal of ordinary income into a glittering treasure trove of wealth. The fate of the weaver of time: Our first challenge is to understand the power of time. Money is not static; it flows like a river, its value decreasing as it moves into the future.

This is the time value of money, the invisible hand that influences every financial decision. We'll learn how to weave the magic of time with the concept of compound interest, where your money not only grows but also earns interest on its own, creating an exponential explosion of wealth over time.

Imagine a small seed, nurtured by compound interest, blossoming into a towering oak tree that brings financial security. Budget Compass: Next, we'll develop a budget, the map that guides our financial journey. It is a tool to track income and expenses, ensuring that we spend less than we earn.

Like a compass guiding a ship, a budget helps us avoid the dangerous waters of overspending and debt. We'll learn how to categorise costs, identify unnecessary leaks, and allocate resources based on our financial goals. The Investment Cauldron: Once we've mastered the art of budgeting, it's time to explore the realm of investing.

This is where we turn our savings into powerful wealth creation tools. We'll look at a variety of investment options, from the steady growth of low-risk assets to the high potential returns (and higher risks) of stocks and other businesses. .

Risk Gloves: But remember, with great potential comes great responsibility. We will equip ourselves with the knowledge to manage risks, understanding the balance between benefits and possible losses. Like a brave knight wearing a gauntlet, we will learn how to protect our financial future from unforeseen dangers.

The Long Game: Financial management and wealth accumulation are not pursuits for the faint of heart. They require discipline, patience and commitment to the long game.

This chapter is not a promise of instant wealth but rather a roadmap for building a secure and prosperous future, one financial brick at a time. So grab your metaphorical shovel and start digging, because the treasure of financial freedom awaits those who are willing to work for it.

1. Conquering money:

Necessary financial skills for entrepreneurship The road to entrepreneurship can be paved with passion but also requires a keen eye for 'a financial warrior'. Here, we equip you with the skills you need to navigate the sometimes treacherous but ultimately rewarding landscape of corporate finance.

The Money Alchemist: The Budget Cauldron: Brews a powerful potion to increase financial awareness through budgeting. This magical document, which meticulously tracks income and expenses, separates the essentials from the frivolous, ensures your resources fuel growth, not madness.

The Ball of the Future: Look into the cash flow crystal ball. Predicting future income and expenses allows you to anticipate difficult situations and take advantage of opportunities, ensuring your business weathers any financial storm.

The Risk Manager's Talisman: Using the Risk Management Talisman, understand the delicate dance between potential rewards and unforeseen pitfalls. This knowledge protects your business from unwise decisions and paves the way for calculated growth.

Master of the Trade: Negotiator's Charm: Refine the art of negotiation, achieving the best possible deals with sellers, partners and investors. Remember, every penny you save is a penny reinvested in your dreams.

The Debt Dragon Slayer: Approach debt with the careful respect it deserves. Understand its power to both build and tear down, use it strategically to grow while avoiding its paralysing embrace.

Savvy Investors: Sowers: Become a master sower by investing your hard-earned profits wisely. Explore different investment options, understand the risk-reward ratio

Explore diverse investment options, understanding the risk-reward spectrum and choosing those that align with your goals and risk tolerance.
The Knowledge Seeker: Never stop learning and growing. The financial landscape is ever-evolving, so stay abreast of market trends, tax regulations, and investment opportunities. This constant learning ensures you remain at the forefront of the financial game.

Remember, mastering these skills equips you not just to survive, but to thrive in the world of entrepreneurial finance. With discipline, knowledge, and a dash of courage, you can transform financial management from a burden to a powerful tool, propelling your venture towards enduring success. So, go forth, brave entrepreneur, and conquer the coin!

2. The Alchemist's Bazaar:

Weaving Revenue Spells for Maximum Profit

Imagine your business as a bustling marketplace, overflowing with vibrant goods and captivating services. But how do you ensure customers flock to your stalls, eager to exchange their hard-earned coin for your offerings? This chapter unveils the secrets of the revenue alchemist, guiding you in concocting potent strategies to generate and maximise profits.

The Art of the Enchanting Offer:
The Alluring Elixir: Craft an irresistible value proposition, the unique blend of benefits that sets your product or service apart. It's the secret ingredient that draws customers in, whispering promises of problem-solving magic or delightful experiences.

The Price Whisperer: Master the art of pricing, striking the delicate balance between value perception and profitability. Consider different pricing models, from subscriptions and freemium options to premium offerings, catering to diverse customer needs and maximising revenue streams.

Expanding Your Reach:
The Customer Magnetism Spell: Employ powerful marketing strategies to draw customers into your orbit. Content marketing, social media wizardry, and targeted advertising are your tools to cast a compelling spell, reaching the right audience and igniting their desire for your offerings.

The Loyalty Potion: Brew a potent customer loyalty potion. Foster strong relationships with existing customers through exceptional service, personalised experiences, and loyalty programs. Remember, a loyal customer is a wellspring of recurring revenue.

Monetization Magic:
The Upselling Charm: Cast the upselling charm, enticing customers to upgrade to higher-tier versions of your product or service, unlocking additional features and increasing their overall spend.

The Cross-Selling Spell: Weave the cross-selling spell, offering complementary products or services alongside your core offerings. This strategic pairing not only increases customer satisfaction but also unlocks new revenue streams.

Optimising the Flow:
The Efficiency Elixir: Don't let inefficiencies drain your profits. Streamline your operations, identify cost-saving opportunities, and leverage technology to improve efficiency. Every penny saved is a penny earned.

The Analytics Oracle: Consult the analytics oracle, harnessing the power of data to understand customer behaviour, identify trends, and measure the effectiveness of your revenue-generating strategies. Data-driven decisions are the key to continuous growth and optimization.

Remember, generating and maximising revenue is an ongoing alchemical process. By mastering these strategies and adapting them to your unique business landscape, you can transform your marketplace into a thriving hub of profit and success. So, unleash your inner revenue alchemist, experiment with these spells, and watch your business flourish!

The Dragon's Treasure: The Investment Strategy of Entrepreneurial Wisdom Successful entrepreneurs are more than just dreamers and builders; they are also wise guardians of their wealth. In this chapter, we explore the dragon's treasure and learn about the investment strategies used by these enterprising individuals to accumulate and protect their wealth.

Calculated risk gambles: A venture capitalist's eye: Entrepreneurs often possess a venture capitalist's unique eye, spotting promising investment opportunities in unexplored territories. They understand the calculated risks involved and approach them with boldness and meticulous diligence.

Diversification Shield: Like a dragon accumulating many treasures, successful entrepreneurs diversify their investments. They spread their wealth across different asset classes, thereby minimizing risk and ensuring long-term financial security. Think of it as a glittering shield, deflecting market fluctuations.

3. Building an Empire Brick by Brick:

Angel Investor Sentiments: Many entrepreneurs become angel investors, nurturing the seeds of promising startups. By supporting innovative businesses, they not only generate potential profits but also establish valuable connections within the startup ecosystem.

Real Estate Alchemist: Entrepreneurs often have a passion for real estate, viewing it as a tangible, income-generating asset. They can invest in rental properties, commercial space or even land development, turning bricks and mortar into a foundation for long-term wealth.

Beyond the Tangible: The Intellectual Investor: Successful entrepreneurs understand that the most valuable investment is often in themselves. They continuously invest in their knowledge and skills by attending seminars, conferences, and continuing their research.

This investment strengthens their advantage and accelerates their entrepreneurial journey, ultimately leading to greater financial rewards. The Legacy Weaver: While accumulating wealth is essential, many entrepreneurs also prioritize building a lasting legacy.

They can invest in philanthropic efforts, social impact projects or educational initiatives, thereby integrating their success into the social fabric. Remember that the investment strategies of successful entrepreneurs are as diverse as their businesses. But by understanding these fundamentals and adapting them to your unique situation, you can start on your own path to building a secure and impactful financial future. So unleash your inner dragon, explore these investment strategies, and watch your wealth grow along with your entrepreneurial spirit.

Chapter 7:

1. **Weavers Guild:** Weaving Bonds to Become Threads of Success In the busy marketplace of life, success often depends on the strength of your bonds, the bonds we create.

This chapter will transform you into a skilled weaver, guiding you to build meaningful relationships that enrich your personal and professional life. The Foundation of Trust: The Thread of Authenticity: The foundation of every strong connection is authenticity.

Be true to yourself, your values and your passions. This authenticity resonates with others, fosters trust, and lays the foundation for lasting relationships.

The Listen Loom: Master the art of active listening. Give the other person your full attention, engage in meaningful dialogue, and seek to understand their perspective. This empathetic approach weaves a trust and connection.

Expand your network: Network: Build a wide network, attend industry events, join professional organisations and connect with people who share your interests . These connections become common threads in the structure of your support system, providing valuable insights and potential collaborations.

The rhythm of reciprocity: Grasping the principle of reciprocity. Offer your time, expertise, and support to others as easily as you seek their support. This promotes balanced and mutually beneficial exchanges, strengthening your relationship.

Strengthens hair strands: Nurtures needles: Relationships, like delicate threads, need to be nurtured. Take time to nurture connections, reach out regularly and offer support and encouragement. This ongoing care ensures that your network remains strong and vibrant.

Gratitude Loom: Express your sincere gratitude for the relationships you have created. A simple thank you or gesture of appreciation goes a long way in strengthening relationships and fostering lasting relationships. Remember that creating meaningful connections is not a one-time action but an ongoing process.

By following these principles and integrating trust, authenticity, and reciprocity into your interaction structure, you can cultivate a network that empowers and supports you on your journey.

To success. So take your metaphorical craft and start creating a life rich with meaningful connections.

1. Alchemist Network:

Turn connections into professional gold Imagine yourself not as a lone figure navigating the career landscape but as an alchemist, using The power of networking to turn your career prospects into something truly valuable. .

In this chapter, we will explore the power of networking and guide you in building a strong professional network that is a gold mine of opportunity, support and personal growth.

The Synergy Stone: The fundamentals of networking lie in the Synergy Stone. Just as combining elements can create something greater than the sum of its parts, connecting with others allows you to share knowledge, ideas and experiences, promoting growth. Common and motivate everyone involved towards their goals.

Source of opportunity: Think of your network as a source of opportunity. By fostering connections with people in your field, you can gain access to more job opportunities, career development opportunities, and collaboration possibilities.

These connections act as your personal career scouts, keeping you informed of hidden gems and opening doors that may otherwise remain closed.
A furnace of knowledge: A strong network is also a furnace of knowledge.

By interacting with people with diverse experiences and perspectives, you can gain access to a wealth of ideas and expertise. You can learn from their successes and failures, gain valuable industry knowledge, and stay ahead of your field.

A haven of support: The career journey can be challenging and a strong network serves as a great source of support. Connecting with like-minded people provides a sense of belonging and community.

You can share your struggles, celebrate your wins and receive invaluable encouragement and advice from those in your network, fostering camaraderie and shared purpose.

Build your network: Building a strong network is not about collecting business cards like trophies. It's about making real connections. Here's how to become a connection alchemist: Be authentic and approachable: Let your true self shine through, making you someone others want to connect with.

Be an active listener: Show genuine interest in others and their experiences. Offer Value: Share your knowledge, expertise, and connections with others. Maintain your relationships: Maintain regular contact, offer support and celebrate each other's successes. Remember that a solid professional network is an investment in your future.

By investing time and effort in building real connections, you will open up a wealth of opportunities, knowledge and support that can propel you towards a successful and fulfilling career. . So start building your own professional network and watch your career turn into something truly golden.

2. Navigator and lighthouse:

Charting a path to meaningful connections Imagine yourself as a navigator, charting a course across a vast ocean of the professional world. Your goal: to reach the key milestones in your industry – the leaders and influencers who illuminate the path to success. This chapter gives you the techniques needed to make meaningful connections with these guiding lights.

Beyond the blinding spotlight: Forget generic emails and empty flattery. To truly connect with industry leaders, you need to look beyond the spotlight. Study their work, understand their values, and identify ways in which your interests and expertise can complement theirs. This authentic approach shows your respect and lays the foundation for a meaningful interaction.

value, don't just look for it: Don't approach industry leaders empty-handed. Give them value. Share your unique ideas, offer to help them with a specific project, or simply engage in an insightful discussion about a topic related to their work.

Remember that connection is a two-way street, and offering value first shows that you're not just looking for personal gain.

Engage authentically: The key to building trust with industry leaders is authenticity. Be genuine in your interactions, express admiration for their work without flattery, and engage in thoughtful conversation.

Let your enthusiasm and passion for your field shine through - these qualities are often more seductive than empty praise. Leverage existing networks: Use your existing network to connect with industry leaders.

Reach out to mutual connections, colleagues, or even alumni networks who may have connections to your target audience. A warm introduction can greatly increase your chances of receiving a meaningful interaction. Become a guide yourself: Remember, building relationships is a long-term game.

Don't expect reciprocity or immediate favours. Instead, focus on yourself as a valuable resource and thought leader in your own right. By actively contributing to your field and building a solid reputation, you will naturally become more famous and attract the attention of industry leaders.

The journey is the reward: The quest to connect with industry leaders is not the immediate outcome. It is a journey of learning, growth and self-improvement. By interacting with these people, you will gain invaluable insights, expand your professional network, and position yourself for future success.

So get on board, pilot and embark on this rewarding journey, armed with these techniques as well as your own passion and perseverance. Remember, a meaningful connection, once established, can light your way for years to come.

3. The Weaver's Web:

Creating connections into a tapestry for Business growth Imagine your business is not a single thread but a living woven from interconnected threads in your network.

In this chapter, we'll show you how to leverage your network to cultivate a thriving ecosystem of connections that will accelerate your business growth and unlock countless opportunities.

Strength in fibres: The basis for leveraging your network lies in its very nature: strength in numbers. Each individual in your network represents a unique segment, with different skills, experiences and perspectives.

By connecting these threads through collaboration, knowledge sharing, and mutual support, you create a powerful website that allows your business to achieve more than it could alone.

Opportunity Loom: Think of your network as an opportunity loom. By fostering connections with potential partners, customers, and advisors, you can reach more leads and collaborate. These connections can open doors to new markets, create valuable referrals and lead to unexpected partnerships that help propel your business forward.

The knowledge: A well-run network acts as a tapestry of knowledge. Each connection provides a unique thread woven with valuable information and expertise. Through open communication and knowledge sharing, you can learn from the successes and failures of others, stay ahead of industry trends, and gain valuable perspectives that help you make informed decisions. business decision.

Weaving the Web: Here's how to become a master weaver and create a network that benefits your business: Be a connector, not just a collector: Promote foster connections between individuals in your network, creating an ecosystem of collaboration and support.

Recommended value first: Before seeking favours, offer your expertise, knowledge or connections to others, building trust and goodwill. Nurture your relationships: Engage regularly with your network, celebrate successes together, and offer support during challenges.

Be an active listener: Pay attention to the needs and interests of others, using your network to connect them with the right opportunities.

The Growth that is running your network is an ongoing process by constantly nurturing relationships and actively seeking collaboration, you weave a tapestry of growth and opportunity that allows your business to thrive in an ever-changing market landscape.

So grab your metaphorical needles, start building your network, and watch your business flourish by leveraging the collective power of your connections.

Chapter 8:

Phoenix Forge:

Where trials turn to triumph The road to success is rarely paved with smooth marble. Usually, it's rough terrain, full of traps and obstacles. This chapter gives you the tools and mindset to tackle these challenges, not as obstacles but as stepping stones on your journey.

We will learn to embrace failure as a catalyst for growth, turning it into the fuel that ignites your phoenix-like rise from the ashes. Forge of Resilience: Imagine challenges like the fire that tempers steel in the forge of resilience. They test your courage, expose your weaknesses and force you to adapt and grow.

By overcoming these challenges, you develop courage, determination, and problem-solving skills that will become invaluable assets as you navigate life's complexities. The Alchemy of Failure: Failure is often demonised, viewed as a sign of weakness. However, in this chapter we represent it as a powerful alchemical ingredient.

Every failure, viewed from the right perspective, constitutes a learning opportunity. It reveals areas for improvement, outlines blind spots, and provides valuable data that can be used to refine your approach and grow stronger. The Flight of the Phoenix: Remember the legendary phoenix, rising from the ashes in a blaze of glory.

This mythical creature embodies the spirit we cultivate in this chapter. We learn to learn from our failures, dust ourselves off and get up with new determination. This resilient spirit becomes the foundation for your future success, motivating you to achieve your goals.

Warrior Mindset:

To successfully overcome challenges, we cultivate a warrior mindset.

This includes: Adopt a growth mindset: Believe that your abilities can be developed and improved through effort and experience. Develop a healthy relationship with failure: See failure as a temporary setback rather than a permanent obstacle. Learn from your mistakes: Take time to analyse your failures and identify areas for improvement.

Build a support network:

Surround yourself with positive and encouraging people who believe in you. Beyond the Battlefield: Remember that overcoming challenges and accepting failure is not only about success but also about personal growth and transformation.

By overcoming difficult situations, you develop your inner strength, resilience and wisdom. These qualities not only benefit your professional life but also enrich your personal journey and help you face every obstacle life brings your way.

So, step into the phoenix forge, embrace the flames of challenges and turn them into the fuel that drives you towards a better future. Remember that the greatest victories are often born from the ashes of defeat.

1. The Entrepreneurial Adventure:

Conquering monsters on the road to success The entrepreneurial journey is a captivating adventure, filled with the promise of uncharted territories discovered and the potential for revolutionary achievements. However, like any epic tale, it is not without its mythical creatures - challenges that threaten to derail even the bravest adventurers.

The Financial Hydra: This many-headed monster rears its ugly head in various forms: lack of initial capital, ensuring the safety of investors and maintaining healthy cash flow.

To beat this hydra, diversify your finances, present a compelling business plan, and prioritise building a sustainable financial model. Remember, financial prudence is your strongest weapon.

Chimera of Uncertainty: This unpredictable creature represents the inherent uncertainty of markets, shifting consumer preferences, and unforeseen economic fluctuations.

To overcome the illusion, be adaptable, conduct in-depth market research, and cultivate a healthy sense of calculated risk-taking. Remember, flexibility is your shield against the unknown.

The Siren Song of Procrastination: This mesmerising song can lull even the most determined businessman into a state of inaction. To combat the siren call, prioritise tasks effectively, set realistic deadlines, and hold yourself accountable. Remember that constant progress, no matter how small, is necessary to overcome inertia.

The Cyclops of Overwork: This one-eyed giant symbolises the relentless pursuit of work, neglecting personal happiness and promoting professional burnout. To tame cyclops, delegate tasks effectively, set healthy boundaries, and prioritise self-care. Remember that a well-rested and balanced businessman will be more productive.

The Sphinx of Self-Doubt: This mysterious creature asks tough questions that can erode confidence and hinder progress. To outsmart the sphinx, surround yourself with a support network, celebrate your achievements, and focus on learning from failures. Remember, confidence is your strongest weapon against self-doubt.

The journey continues: These mythical creatures represent just some of the challenges that may arise during your entrepreneurial journey. However, by understanding their forms and using the right tools – resourcefulness, adaptability, resilience and confidence – you can overcome these challenges and win. win.

Remember, the greatest entrepreneurial stories are not about the absence of obstacles but about the courage and determination to overcome them. So embark on your adventure, armed with these legendary ideas, and chart your own path to success.

2. The Alchemist's Crucible:

Turn Failure into a Philosopher's Stone The path to success, like a winding mountain road, is rarely easy. Failures and mistakes are often scattered along the way, tempting us to turn back. What if we saw these obstacles not as obstacles but as the alchemist's crucible? In this fiery furnace we can turn the lead of failure into the philosopher's stone of success.

Lessons from the Ashes: Failure, although painful, has a unique alchemical quality: it reveals our weaknesses. It exposes flaws in our planning, flaws in our execution, and areas where knowledge is lacking.

By accepting this uncomfortable truth, we gain invaluable insights that fuel our growth. We learn from past mistakes, to prevent them from becoming future mistakes.

The Rebirth of the Phoenix: Every failure, seen through the right lens, becomes a phoenix feather. This ignites the fire of determination, igniting a new passion to rise from the ashes. This new determination drives us forward, pushing us to refine our approach, develop new strategies and emerge stronger than before.

The Master's Path: Every successful individual has a story woven from failures. The difference lies not in the absence of missteps but in the subsequent transformation. They view failure not as a sign of incompetence but as a stepping stone on the path to mastery. They accept the lessons it brings, rise up with new purpose and ultimately conquer their goals.

The Alchemist's Hand: So how can we use the alchemist's hand and turn failure into success? Here are the essential ingredients: Seize learning opportunities: Actively investigate what happened. Analyse your mistakes, identify the root causes, and learn from them.

Develop a growth mindset: Believe that your abilities can be developed and improved through effort and experience. Maintain a positive attitude: Don't let failures define you. Focus on lessons learned and opportunities for improvement.

Find support: Surround yourself with positive, encouraging people who believe in you and can guide you.

Beyond the Crucible: Remember that The Alchemist's Crucible is not just about success but about personal transformation.

By accepting failure and learning from it, we cultivate resilience, self-awareness, and adaptability. These qualities become not only tools for success but also the essence of a fulfilling and growth-oriented life. So, next time you encounter failure, don't despair.

Step into the alchemist's crucible, accept the heat and turn it into the fuel that will help you achieve your greatest achievements. Remember that the greatest successes often start from the embers of failure.

3. The Navigator and the Storm:

Weathering the Storms of Adversity Imagine you are a seasoned navigator, charting a course across the ocean vastness of life. You will certainly encounter storms – times of difficulty, loss and uncertainty.

This chapter guides you through essential strategies for staying resilient and motivated during these challenging times, ensuring you reach your destination with unwavering determination.

Anchors of Hope: The first line of defence against the fury of the storm is to strengthen your anchors of hope.

These anchors represent your values, purpose, and long-term goals. By holding fast to these guiding principles, you maintain a sense of direction and purpose, even when the winds of adversity threaten to blow you off course.

A beacon of self-care: In the midst of a chaotic storm, it's easy to neglect ourselves. However, self-care is a beacon that guides you through the darkness. Prioritise activities that nourish your mind, body, and spirit. This can include exercise, healthy eating, sleep hygiene, and practising mindfulness.

A person who is well-rested and focused will be better equipped to weather the challenges of the storm. Support crew: No navigator travels alone. Surround yourself with a team of supportive people who encourage, understand and provide practical help during difficult times.

These could be friends, family, mentors, or even support groups. Sharing your struggles and triumphs with others fosters a sense of connection and belonging, reminding you that you're not alone in weathering the storm.

Gratitude Compass: Even in times of trouble, there is always something to be grateful for. Cultivating an attitude of gratitude acts as your compass, reminding you of life's blessings, no matter how small.

This practice shifts your focus from what you lack to the abundance around you, promoting resilience and a positive attitude. The resilience of the reed: Remember that true resilience is not about remaining rigid and inflexible in the face of adversity.

Like a reed, it bends without breaking. Learn to adapt to changing circumstances, adjust your sails as needed, and find new ways to work toward your goals. Behind the Storm: Life's storms, although difficult, are only temporary. By using these strategies, you will not only be free from trauma but also strengthened and empowered.

You gain valuable wisdom, develop a deeper appreciation of your inner strengths, and discover a new sense of resilience that prepares you for future challenges. So hold on to your anchor, find refuge in the beacon of self-care, lean on your support team, sail with the compass of gratitude, and remember the reed's resilience.

With these tools, you can weather any storm and come out the other side, ready to continue your journey on calmer seas.

Chapter 9:

Problem-solving Alchemist's Playground: Brewing Disruptive Innovation in a Cauldron of Stagnation Industries, like boiling cauldrons, can stagnate over time. Innovation, the alchemist's secret ingredient, is the key to escaping the mundane and creating a powerful elixir of disruption. In this chapter, we will explore the art and science of revolutionizing industries and infusing them with a new wave of innovation and progress.

Beyond the familiar potion: The formula for success often employed by established industries can become a familiar, comforting, but ultimately stifling potion. This resistance to change causes stagnation, hinders growth, and makes them vulnerable to new innovators.

Disruption Catalysts: Disruption Catalysts are the spark that lights the fire of innovation.

This can take many forms: a new technology, a completely new business model or even a change in consumer behavior. This catalyst disrupts the established order, forcing industries to adapt or find themselves irrelevant. Alchemist's Tools: So how do you become a disruptive alchemist?

Here are the essential tools:

Challenge the status quo: Question every existing assumption, tradition and practice in your industry. Constantly ask "why" and "how", looking for opportunities for improvement.

Embrace experimentation: Don't be afraid to experiment and fail. Failure is often a springboard toward breakthrough innovation.

Escape from the Cauldron: Find inspiration in a variety of fields and professions. Look beyond the familiar to find unique solutions and new perspectives.

Promote Collaboration: Promote a culture of open communication and collaboration that encourages diversity of perspectives and collective problem solving.

The Power of Disruption: Disruption, while painful for established players, can ultimately benefit entire industries. It: Increase competition: Create a more dynamic and competitive environment, bringing better products, services and prices to consumers.

Drive innovation: drives a race to the top, pushing all players to constantly innovate and improve their services. Empowering New Players: opens the door to new entrants who can bring new perspectives and challenge the dominance of established players.

Beer brewing process: Disrupting an industry is not a one-time event; it is an ongoing process. The alchemist must continually experiment, improve his recipes, and adapt to changing market dynamics.

Beyond the Cauldron: Remember that pursuing disruption isn't just about disrupting industries; it's about creating positive change.

By using innovation as a force for good, we can build a more sustainable, equitable and prosperous future for everyone. So, unleash your inner alchemist, grab your metaphorical cauldron and start brewing.

The power to create positive disruption awaits you, and with the right ingredients and a little courage, you can become the architect of meaningful change in your industry.

1. **The Alchemist's Wager:** Break through the market and achieve success Imagine the business scene is a bustling market, stalls filled with familiar products. But among these predictable offerings, the most prominent is a lone businessman, the Alchemist.

Their location sparkles with the promise of something radically new, a powerful elixir of innovation and breakthrough. This chapter explores the importance of these factors in business success.

1. Stagnation of stagnation:

Many established businesses, lulled by the comfort of familiar formulas, fall into stagnation. Their services become predictable, their processes become fixed, leaving them vulnerable to the winds of change. This stasis is fertile ground for disruption and opportunity for the alchemist.

The Elixir of Disruption: The Elixir of Disruption is a powerful combination of novelty and ingenuity. This can take many forms: a revolutionary product, a revolutionary service or even a radical change in the way business is done.

This elixir disrupts the established order, forcing competitors to adapt and consumers to become aware of it. The Alchemist's Arsenal: Successful alchemists have a unique arsenal: The Quill Pen: They constantly challenge the status quo, questioning every assumption and tradition in their preferred field.

Their constant "why" and "how" questions became the foundation for revolutionary ideas. The Experimental Still: They take calculated risks and experiments. For them, failure is not the end but a stepping stone on the path of revolutionary innovation.

Inspirational Lens: They look beyond the boundaries of their industry, drawing inspiration from diverse fields and perspectives. This unique approach sparks new ideas and ignites the creative fire.

The Cup of Collaboration: They foster a culture of open communication and collaboration, welcoming diverse perspectives and encouraging collective problem solving. This collaborative spirit unleashes their team's collective genius. The

Power of Disruption: Although initially groundbreaking, the Alchemist's Elixir eventually benefits the entire market: Increased Competition: Dynamic landscape and Competition encourages innovation, leading to the best products, services and prices for consumers.

Unlock Innovation: Disruption triggers a race to the top, pushing all players to constantly improve and refine their products. Empowering new players: Disruption creates opportunities for new entrants with fresh perspectives, challenging the dominance of established players.

Brewing in progress: Disruption is not a one-time action but a continuous process. The alchemist must constantly tinker with his formula, adapt to changing market dynamics, and improve his product.

Beyond the market: The pursuit of innovation and breakthrough goes beyond mere commercial success. This becomes a catalyst for positive change. By harnessing these strengths, entrepreneurs can create a more sustainable, equitable and prosperous future for all.

So if you're looking to dominate the market, take on the role of alchemist. Experiment, challenge, collaborate and disrupt. With the right combination of innovation and a little courage, you can create your medicine of success and leave your mark on the world.

2. Uncovering the market's gems: Innovation Strategy Innovation thrives on fertile soil and that fertile soil often hides loopholes – Market gaps are waiting to be discovered. But how can you become a creative archaeologist, adept at discovering these gems?

Here are some unique tactics:

1. Become a frustrated detective:

Instead of just observing customers, embrace their frustrations. Follow them in their daily activities, listen carefully to their complaints, and become their problem-solving partner. What minor inconveniences interrupt their progress? What tasks make them yearn for a better way of doing things?

By channeling your inner detective and investigating these frustrations, you'll uncover opportunities for solutions that truly resonate.

2. Embrace the power of "What if?

" » : Don't be afraid to challenge the status quo. Ask yourself: "What if…?
" » Then let your imagination run wild. What if traditional office spaces could transform to meet the needs of a nomadic workforce?
What if our exercise routines seamlessly integrate with our daily activities?

By considering these "what ifs," you push the boundaries of existing solutions and pave the way for breakthrough innovation.

3. Borrow from the unexpected:

Look beyond your immediate industry for inspiration. Explore seemingly unrelated areas and see if there are transferable solutions to explore. Perhaps a technique used in the video game industry could be applied to revolutionize education.

Perhaps an environmentally friendly solution can be applied to improve production efficiency. By combining ideas from many different fields, you can create unexpected and ingenious solutions.

4. Appreciate the wisdom of the crowd: Innovation is not a solitary act. Harness the collective intelligence of your community. Host brainstorming sessions fueled by diverse perspectives. Collect ideas through online platforms.

By tapping into the collective intelligence of the crowd, you can uncover hidden corners and unleash a wave of creative solutions.

5. Prototype with playful curiosity:

Don't be afraid to get your hands dirty and experiment. Create low-fidelity prototypes using off-the-shelf materials.

Test them with real users, collect feedback, and iterate quickly. This playful approach allows you to explore possibilities without getting bogged down in the complexities of perfectionism.

Remember that innovation is a journey, not a destination. By applying these unique strategies, you can become a skilled archaeologist of market gaps, uncover hidden opportunities, and develop innovative solutions that truly make a difference special.

3. Giants of transformation:

Stories of breakthrough entrepreneurs The business landscape is littered with the ruins of once-mighty companies destroyed by the tide constant innovation.

But amidst the ruins, giants do not have brute strength but breakthrough genius. These Transformation Titans are entrepreneurs who dare to challenge the status quo and reshape entire industries. Let's learn the interesting stories of some of the pioneers:

1. **Robin Hood of ride-sharing services:** Travis Kalanick (Uber) In the field of overpriced taxis, Kalanick has established himself be a rebel with an . By leveraging the sharing economy and the power of smartphones, Uber has democratized transportation, providing convenient and affordable rides at the touch of a button. Traditional taxi companies, once considered untouchable, have had to adapt to Uber's swift and decisive disruption.

2. **The Hospitality Heretic:** Brian Chesky and Joe Gebbia (Airbnb) Hospitality, the undisputed leaders in the lodging sector, face an unexpected challenge when Chesky and Gebbia dare to revolutionize hospitality guest.

Airbnb, their brainchild, opened the doors to a global network of unique and affordable accommodation options. Travelers have embraced the authentic experiences and personalized connections offered by Airbnb, forcing hotels to rethink their strategies in the changed landscape.

3. **Streaming Wizard:** Reed Hastings (Netflix) In the age of video rental, Hastings cast a powerful spell with Netflix. His vision of on-demand entertainment, delivered seamlessly over the Internet, disrupted the movie rental industry with a virtual click. Traditional video stores, once ubiquitous, have become a relic of the past as consumers flock to the vast and convenient library offered by Netflix.

4. **Electric Evangelist**: Elon Musk (Tesla) Under the dominance of gas-guzzling giants, Musk emerged as a prophet of electric mobility. Tesla, its vehicle of change, has challenged the hegemony of traditional automakers by launching elegant and efficient electric vehicles.

Tesla not only redefined the perception of electric cars, but also sparked a global debate on sustainability, forcing the entire auto industry to reconsider its fuel-based foundation. These are just a few stories from the epic saga of groundbreaking entrepreneurs.

Their story is a powerful reminder that innovation can emerge from the most unexpected angles and that even the oldest industries are vulnerable to the winds of change. As we move into the future, the business landscape will undoubtedly continue to evolve, shaped by those with bold visions who dare to challenge norms and disrupt the status quo.

Chapter 10:

Sowing the seeds of change: Planting the legacy of success Success, like a magnificent tree, casts a long shadow. But the real satisfaction lies not only in the heights it reaches but also in the seeds it plants and the lasting legacy it leaves behind.

This chapter delves deeper into the profound act of giving back and explores how you can cultivate a legacy that goes beyond your personal achievements.

1. From Consumer to Contributor:

We often begin our journey as consumers, passively absorbing the fruits of the world around us. However, the real growth lies in moving towards contributor status. Look beyond your immediate needs and identify areas where your skills, resources, or even just your time can have a positive impact.

Whether it's mentoring a young mind, volunteering for a cause you care about, or simply showing kindness in daily interactions, every contribution, no matter how small, has power. Strongly spreads outward, creating a chain reaction that brings positive change.

Find a reason to give:

Giving back is more than just checking a box; it's about connecting with a deeper purpose. What ignites a spark in you? Is it the environment, education, social justice or something else? Identifying your "why" will fuel your passion and guide you toward goals that align with your core values.

Beyond the obvious: Unique giving:

The act of giving doesn't always require grand gestures or enormous resources. Sometimes the most impactful contributions are those that are unique.

Sharing your knowledge by offering free workshops, using your platform to raise awareness for social causes, or simply listening to those in need are all ways strong to make a difference.

The Ripple Effect: Building an Inspiring Legacy: Remember that your legacy is not just what you achieve but also the impact you have on others. By actively contributing to improving your community and the world around you, you inspire others to do the same.

This ripple effect, triggered by your act of giving, has the ability to create lasting positive change, far beyond your own life. The Final Bloom: A Life Beyond Success As you travel the path to success, remember that true satisfaction lies in sowing the seeds of change.

By giving back, you cultivate a legacy that goes beyond personal success, leaving a lasting impact that enriches the lives of others and thrives in a world full of positive change. So embrace your role as a contributor, find your unique "why" for giving, and embark on a journey to create a legacy that resonates far beyond the limits of your own success by Building the bridges, not walls:

The alchemy of charity Imagine society as a large mosaic. Each individual receives a tile, contributing its color and texture to the overall image. But what happens when some of the tiles fall off, leaving behind gaps that threaten the integrity of the entire piece?

Philanthropy becomes the mortar, the essential force that unites us, filling these gaps and creating a more vibrant and resilient society. Philanthropy is not just about throwing money at problems;

it's a question of alchemy. It is the transformation of resources – time, talent or treasure – into positive change. It's about realizing that our success is intimately linked to the well-being of the communities around us.

When we give, we: Bridge the gap: Philanthropy helps us connect with people facing challenges, fostering empathy and understanding. This allows us to build bridges where walls once stood, creating a more inclusive and equitable society.

Spark Innovation: Philanthropy can be a catalyst for revolutionary ideas. By supporting innovative solutions, we empower individuals and organizations to solve complex problems creatively.

Cultivating Hope: A helping hand, a scholarship opportunity, access to health care – these acts of charity can sow seeds of hope, reminding individuals and communities that they are not alone and that they can have a better future.

The impact of philanthropy is expanding: Empowerment potential: By investing in education and skills training, we equip people with the tools they need to reach their full potential its potential. This in turn strengthens the workforce and spurs economic growth.

Symphony of Change:
Philanthropy empowers diverse voices and fosters collaboration among individuals, organizations and governments. This collective action creates a symphony of change, solving problems that no single entity can solve alone.

Leave a Legacy: Our time on this earth is limited, but through philanthropy we can leave a lasting impact. We can shape the world for future generations, ensuring a brighter picture for all.

Charity is not a burden; it's an investment. It is an investment in a stronger, fairer and more dynamic society. It's about recognizing the interconnectedness of our world and choosing to actively participate in improving it. So let's close the gap, ignite innovation and nurture hope – through the power of philanthropy.

2. Integrating Purpose with Profit:

Developing a Socially Responsible Business Model In today's landscape, consumers are increasingly looking to regulate their spending them according to their values.

Companies that prioritize social responsibility, beyond just making a profit, not only do well but also gain a strategic advantage. Here are some unique strategies for embedding purpose into your business model:

1. **Embrace radical transparency:** Don't be afraid to lift the veil on your operations. Share your supply chain practices, environmental footprint, and commitment to social good. This radical transparency promotes trust with customers who value sustainable and ethical practices.

2. **Reinvent your value chain:** Look beyond traditional models and rethink your entire value chain from a societal perspective. Can you source material ethically?
Can you reduce your carbon footprint through innovative manufacturing or packaging methods? Can you empower local communities through fair business practices? By integrating social responsibility into every step of your operations, you will create a virtuous circle of positive impact.

3. **The power of purposeful collaboration**: Collaboration is essential. Collaborate with organizations that share your values and leverage their expertise to amplify your social impact. This could involve co-creating products with a social purpose, collaborating on community development initiatives, or even supporting employee volunteer programs.

4. **Breakthrough from within:** Empower your employees to become champions of social responsibility. Encourage them to identify opportunities in their roles to make a positive

difference. This could involve anything from developing energy saving initiatives in the office to volunteering for social activities.

5. Measure what matters: Don't just talk, follow through and measure your impact. Develop clear metrics to track progress toward your social responsibility goals. This could involve measures related to reducing carbon emissions, increasing community engagement or employee volunteer hours. By quantifying your impact, you can demonstrate your commitment and hold yourself accountable for creating positive change.

Remember that social responsibility is not a one-time effort; it is a continuous journey. By applying these strategies, you can embed purpose into the DNA of your business model, creating a sustainable, socially responsible business that thrives while making a difference exceptionally positive in the world.

3. Carve your mark on the time:

Leave a legacy of inspiration Success, like a shooting star, leaves a temporary glow in the night sky.

But real satisfaction lies in something much more lasting: a legacy that inspires future generations. It is your invitation to mark your story in time, leaving a mark that not only resonates throughout the corridors of your own achievements but also ignites the fire of ambition in future entrepreneurs.

1. From Achievement to Alchemy: Don't settle for just accumulating awards. Instead, turn your achievements into an alchemist's brew, a potent mixture of lessons learned, wisdom gained, and challenges to be overcome.

Share your story through mentoring programs, workshops, or even engaging autobiographies. By providing insight into your journey, you give aspiring entrepreneurs the roadmap, compass, and courage to navigate their own business missions.

2. Sow the seeds of innovation: Beyond sharing your story, become a catalyst for innovation.

Set up incubation programs or seed funding initiatives to nurture the ideas of budding entrepreneurs. Provide your expertise and guidance, helping them refine their concepts and solve the complex problems of turning their vision into reality. By sowing seeds of innovation, you are cultivating fertile ground for the next generation of pioneers to thrive.

3. **Champion collaboration, not competition**: The startup landscape is not a battlefield; It's a collaborative Strengthen partnerships with other successful entrepreneurs, sharing resources and expertise to solve industry-wide challenges.

By fostering a spirit of collaboration rather than competition, you create a supportive ecosystem where aspiring entrepreneurs can learn from the collective wisdom of established leaders.

4. **Lead by example, not by edict**: Remember that actions speak louder than words. Live your values with unwavering integrity, demonstrating the ethical and responsible practices you want to see passed on to future generations of entrepreneurs.

As you navigate the complexities of business, choose integrity over shortcuts, sustainability over exploitation, and purpose over mere profit. Your exemplary behavior will become a beacon, guiding aspiring entrepreneurs to navigate the ethical compass of the business world.

5. **Leave a legacy of strength**, not just achievement: Your legacy should not be determined solely by your personal achievements. Strive to empower others to reach their full potential.

Champion diversity and inclusion in the business landscape, ensuring that ambitious individuals from all backgrounds have the opportunity to contribute their unique talents and perspectives.

By empowering others, you not only enrich the present but also shape a future filled with diverse voices and innovative solutions. Leaving a lasting legacy is not self-aggrandizement; it is intended to light the way for those who follow.

By applying these strategies, you can turn your success into inspiration, ignite the entrepreneurial spirit of generations to come, and ensure that your mark on time to come is more than just not only a fleeting shimmering light but also a beacon for the future.

Conclusion

Much different wealth Awaken the symphony within: The final note of your entrepreneurial journey Entrepreneurship, like a symphony, requires a chorus of multi-instrumentalists form – ambition, tenacity and a firm belief that your melody alone has the power .

To create buzz. This concluding note serves as a final culmination, a reminder of the important agreements that will guide you on your entrepreneurial journey. Remember that you are not alone. The world is full of ambitious individuals, each with a song waiting to be sung.

Encourage collaboration because the combined melody of diverse perspectives creates a stronger and more impactful symphony. Don't be afraid of discord. Challenges and failures are inevitable, but they are also important considerations that add depth and dimension to your business.

Learn from them, adapt and become stronger. Let passion be the conductor. It is the driving force that will fuel your perseverance and ignite the fire of innovation. Pursue your dreams with relentless enthusiasm, let your passion lead you to a complete and impressive symphony of success.

Finally, never stop creating. The entrepreneurial journey is a continuous evolution, a never-ending song with endless possibilities for growth and impact. Enjoy the power of learning, constantly seek new knowledge and hone your skills.

By applying these notes, you can unleash your inner entrepreneurial symphony, leaving a lasting legacy that resonates not only for your personal success but also for change The positivity you inspire in the world around you. So take a deep breath, raise your instrument and start composing the symphony of your dreams.

1. **Hidden gems revealed:** A treasure chest of wealth creation strategies The book opens like a captivating treasure map, guiding you to hidden treasures – the secrets to creating wealth. Check out the key strategies he reveals:

1. **Become an "unconventional detective":** Don't just observe the financial landscape; Take on the role of detective. Uncover hidden opportunities by examining your own spending habits and the frustrations of those around you. What financial problems need solutions? By unleashing your inner detective, you can identify market gaps and develop creative solutions that unlock your wealth creation potential.

2. **Practice "What if?**
" » Thoughts: Don't be afraid to challenge the status quo. Ask yourself: "What if…?
" » and unleash your imagination. What if traditional investment strategies could be revolutionized by technology?

What if everyday tasks could be monetized using innovative platforms? By considering these "what ifs," you push the boundaries of conventional thinking and open the door to unique paths to wealth creation.

3. **Embrace the power of "unexpected connections":** Look beyond your immediate scope of inspiration. Explore seemingly unrelated industries and see if there are transferrable wealth secrets waiting to be discovered.

Perhaps gaming industry marketing strategies can be adapted to increase profits for your local business. By combining ideas from many different fields, you can create rich and unexpected paths.

4. **Leveraging the "wisdom of the crowd"**: Creating wealth is not a solo effort. Harness the collective intelligence of your community. Hold brainstorming sessions with diverse perspectives to explore hidden financial perspectives.

Use online platforms to gather ideas and gather valuable feedback. By tapping into the collective intelligence of the public, you can expand your horizons and identify unique paths to financial success.

5. **Embrace "fun experimentation"**: Don't be afraid to get your hands dirty and experiment. Develop low-cost prototypes of your financial ideas and test them with real people. Collect feedback and iterate quickly.

This interesting approach allows you to explore many different wealth creation strategies without getting bogged down in the complexities of perfectionism. Remember that this book does not offer a single, sure path to wealth.

Instead, it provides you with a treasure trove of diverse strategies, encouraging you to adapt them to your own circumstances and ignite your own entrepreneurial spirit. So, grab your metaphorical shovel, apply these unique tactics, and start discovering your hidden wealth-building potential.

2. **Adventure awaits:** Embark on your wealth creation journey The final page has been turned, but the real adventure – the wealth creation journey your own – just getting started. This book, like a reliable travel guide, has equipped you with knowledge and strategies, but the most important step awaits us: actions.

Think of this book as a treasure map, its ink revealing hidden paths to financial success. But just having a card is not enough; you must leave the beaten path, compass in hand, and embark on your own exploration. There will be challenges, detours, and moments of doubt, but with every step you take, the treasure you seek – financial security and fulfillment – will come closer.

Remember these guiding principles as you begin your journey: Embrace the unknown: The path to wealth creation is rarely linear. Be prepared to explore uncharted territory and be open to the unexpected.

Drive your passion: Let your inner drive be the engine that drives you forward. When challenges arise, remember the "why" behind your quest. Celebrate every milestone: Recognize and celebrate your wins, big or small. These recognized moments will keep you motivated and allow you to move forward.

Learn from every failure: See failure not as an obstacle but as an opportunity to grow. Analyze what went wrong, adjust your approach, and become stronger. Share your story: Inspire others by sharing your experiences and lessons learned.

Your journey can become a beacon of hope and a guide for those with ambitions to create wealth. The world is waiting for your unique contribution. Take the knowledge gleaned from this book, combine it with your own ingenuity and determination, and embark on your wealth-building adventure.

Remember that the greatest treasure is not always found at the end of the journey but in the growth, resilience and sense of accomplishment you gain along the way. So, boldly step into the unknown, take on challenges, and chart your own path to financial freedom and fulfillment.

3. Goodbye, fellow pioneers:

A spark ignites the entrepreneurial spirit in you This book is not just a collection of words; it is a compass that guides you toward your business North Star.

Now that you close the final page, the real journey begins: a grand expedition into the unexplored territories of your dreams. But before you go, let these last sparks of inspiration light the fire within:

With the following benefits below

1. **Dream in Technicolor, not grayscale:** Don't be satisfied with timid aspirations. Paint your dreams in vibrant colors, full of ambition, innovation and a touch of daring. Remember that the world is hungry for bold ideas and breakthrough solutions.

2. **Embrace the symphony of discomfort**: The road to success is rarely paved with rose petals. It will be filled with challenges, failures and moments of doubt. But these inconveniences are the necessary chords that create your symphony of success. Learn to accept them, for they are the catalyst for growth and resilience.

3. **Let curiosity be your guide:** Never stop asking questions, exploring possibilities and venturing beyond your comfort zone. Curiosity is the fuel that drives innovation and keeps your entrepreneurial spirit burning.

4. **Celebrate detours:** The road to your destination may not be a straight line. Take detours because they often lead to unexpected discoveries, valuable connections, and hidden opportunities.

5. **Leave your mark on time:** Don't just pursue financial success; strive to have a positive impact. Your weave

www.ingramcontent.com/pod-product-compliance
Lightning Source LLC
Chambersburg PA
CBHW070355230526
45471CB00006B/2574